DISCLAIMER:

This book contains general information based on my own knowledge and personal experiences and is written solely from my perspective. I have tried to recreate events, locales, and conversations from my memories of them. In order to maintain anonymity, I have not used any individual names and other identifying characteristics of people and places from my story.

Marissa 🙂

Be Blessed
Be Encouraged
Jer. 29:11

Adler "Chocolate" Watson
9/18

DEDICATION

First, I give all the praise to my Lord and Savior
Jesus Christ!
In Him, I'm saved, free, and REDEEMED!

A special dedication to my number one supporter,
husband, and best friend, Kevin Watson, and, to
the sunshine of my heart, my daughter, Archesicia
"Tweety" Thomas. Also, thanks to my dear friend,
Gail Mallery, who worked day and night helping me
put this book together, who encouraged me to let
go and be free, who cried with me when writing
was hard, but most of all who loved me when I
struggled with loving myself. Thanks to Jill Marr
with "Red Stick Creative" for using her talent to
design a beautiful cover and for all the many things
she does to support Redeemed Women. These,
along with a host of friends and family have
supported the call on my life, and spent days and
nights praying for me and encouraging me. Thank
you all!

It is my hope that you, the reader, will be
encouraged by the stories from my life and will see
in them the call God has placed on me. Find in
God the way to be a survivor in your own life no
matter what pain or obstacles you face. I was
counted out a long time ago; but today I realize I
am anointed by God for His purpose and I survived
to share my path to redemption with you!

"In Him was life, and the life was the light of men. The light shines in the darkness, and the darkness has not overcome it."

John 1: 4-5

PREFACE

I heard a sermon during a time of great pain and loss in my life due to a series of bad choices I made combined with events out of my control. I was broken, in pain, and had lost hope. In this sermon the priest said, "Go back to the places you said no to God, and ask Him to redeem them." So, I did. Over the next few months, as God revealed those places to me one by one, the power of redemption overcame each and every one…and still does. People and situations were put in my path, and I drew from those experiences to speak wisdom and truth into their lives and to anyone who needed to hear it. I experienced the full circle of God's amazing grace, mercy, and redemption. As I began working with my dear friend, Chocolate, on her story I realized that this sermon needed to expand to," wherever you have brokenness and pain, wherever evil has touched your life, wherever there is great loss…ask God to redeem those places and trust Him with those places; and, His light will overcome the darkness and He will redeem them."

We are all broken. We all have pain. We have all said no to God in some facet of our lives and we all are in need of redemption. From abortion, addiction, or adultery to less subtle yet powerful dark places as judging others, gossip, and pride…God's light overcomes them all. He can and will take any dark place in our lives and redeem it. We only need to lay it at the cross and ask God, and He will. That hidden place we don't talk about, that pain we haven't shared with anyone, the abuse we have been silent about and kept buried...trust Him. Our Father, who loves us unconditionally, will redeem, revive, restore, and renew us. He will use the wrong, the suffering, and the pain in our lives, and give us the opportunity to shine light on someone else's darkness and experience God's mercy and grace on their lives.

As you read Chocolate's story, my prayer is you will see the power of God and how He was there with her from the beginning. He was with her in her tears and cries for help. He was with her in her pain. He was with her when evil tried to stamp out her life. May her story not only shed light on the overwhelming obstacles women face who live in poverty every day; but also, expose the wounds in your own life that are in need of healing. Evil has no socioeconomic barriers, nor does pain, suffering, or hopelessness. Likewise, there are no boundaries for God's steadfast love and forgiveness! There are no barriers for anyone in need of redemption!

Chocolate's whole life is an ongoing story of healing and restoration. She has taken those places of pain and despair and trusted God to redeem them, and oh how He has! Her story is a sermon of redemption, mercy, forgiveness, and grace. She is a light shining in the darkness. She is an "Anointed Survivor" and a Redeemed Woman on fire for God!

Gail Mallery
Board President, Redeemed Women

"Overcoming poverty is not a gesture of charity. It is the protection of a fundamental human right; the right to dignity and a decent life."

Nelson Mandela

CHAPTER 1

I really don't remember anything prior to my third birthday. Up until that point, I know only the basics. I was born July 12, 1981 at Parkland Hospital in Dallas, TX. My mom and dad named me Aelicia Ann Simpson. My mom was a drug addict and my dad was an alcoholic who also had Cerebral Palsy, so, there was no celebration welcoming me into this world. There were no baby showers or well wishes for the new couple and their new baby. I was another black baby born to a junkie.

It didn't take long for my parents to divorce. Mom was 18 and my Dad was 21 when I was born and by my second birthday, they split. Dad got custody of me being as my mom was on drugs, but, that was just on paper. Mom came by and picked me up and took me off with her to California. I was two years old. We moved in with my great aunt and my grandmother. They were on drugs too...go figure. I can't tell you a thing about the house, the neighborhood, nothing. I must have lived and breathed; because I am still here, but that's all. I was invisible. There are no cute baby albums of me or stories of my first steps or words. As a child, I must have learned to walk and talk, because I made it to my third birthday, and I DO remember that day.

Mom brought me back to Dallas for a year and tried to make another go of it with my dad. My cousin was having a birthday party at Sesame Street and we shared the party. It was the first time I remember being around other children and the first time I remember being noticed. Maybe because that big yellow bird coming at me scared the crap out of me and I screamed to the top of my lungs. Cookie Monster and the rest of them were equally terrifying. But, in spite of that, I remember it was a good day...until mom and my aunt got into a fist fight in the street outside over the shoes my mom had put on me.

We went back to California and back into darkness. All I remember are images. Sleeping on floors, rats, roaches, dirt, no electricity, no food, showers, water...just shelter and never the same place for long. Mom would sell drugs, sell her body, steal, and rob people for drugs. Not to feed me, but, to feed her habit. Sometimes she took me with her; other times, she left me with strangers. Sometimes she would find a dealer to hook up with, and we would get new clothes or shoes. She was with one for a while that was a big -time dealer in Hollywood and was part of the mafia. We got all kinds of things then, but, it didn't last long.

BUT GOD:

The reality is, in the United States, children are born every day into conditions far worse than mine. Giving me up was never a consideration. In fact, in my community adoption is not even considered an option. Nor is abortion. Having children is part of life. So even though my parents were not equipped in any way to be parents by most people's standards, there was love present and I was wanted. Even though my mother's mind was a prisoner to drugs, in her own way she tried to raise me in a world balanced by her need to take care of me and her driving need for her next fix. Not once did she want to give me up to anyone. She wanted to care for me, and in her mind, clouded by drugs, she did. She was simply living out what she had experienced as well as the two generations before them. I am the third generation born into poverty in the United States. And so it is for thousands of children born into generational poverty every year. The cycle runs so deep that the reality of what a person in this environment needs to survive is much different from what is portrayed in TV sitcoms and even the best documentary television shows. Until society understands the depth of the issues, the cycles cannot be broken. Generational poverty is a culture complete with its own set of rules of conduct, what is acceptable or not, and with walls built so high and deep that not even the government or all the Ivy League graduates in our country have been able to penetrate them and understand what the true issues are. I have seen so many people, who mean well, tell us what we need...but they never bother to ask. Countless programs, a lot of money, welfare and others are all band-aids and actually perpetuate some of the problems we face. We are a sub-culture in America that needs to change its direction from the inside out. We do not need to change *who we are* but gain stability long enough to embrace the best in our culture and eradicate the bad. This will not happen overnight and it will take multiple agencies and ministries working together, *coming along side* us, listening and hearing us and then working with us for solutions. See *our* world through *our* eyes and together, help us build leaders within our communities and help us thrive.

The Bible gives us a picture of what this looks like. Early Christians were, for the most part, considered outcasts. All of a sudden there were Jews, Romans, Greeks, Gentiles, Samaritans ...all thrown into together in a community in the midst of one of the most violent times in human history. They formed a community that, even though they risked their lives to be a member, had people wanting to join them in massive numbers. Why?

The people supported each other and helped each other. They were neighbors to each other. They were united in their faith in God and worked together to build their community. They had very little but by sharing among themselves and coming together, their community began to thrive, and they had hearts of joy and generosity.

This is what I have been anointed by God to bring to my community and hopefully beyond. I have a vision to meet the women in my community where they are and show them Jesus. And, as we meet needs together and learn to trust and support each other, we will change our community from the inside out. We will be the light of Dallas and a model of God's grace and beauty in a world of darkness.

"Loneliness and the feeling of being unwanted is the most terrible poverty."

Mother Teresa

CHAPTER 2

Mom did all kinds of drugs: PCP, heroin, crack, pot, meth...whatever she could get her hands on; she wasn't too picky. She paid for drugs with prostitution, robbery, dealing...whatever she needed to do to get her fix. My brother was born during this time and I became a parent at age four. I took care of him and protected him as much as a 4-year-old child could. Mom taught me how to open a can with a knife so we could eat right out of the can. She even taught me how to make drugs. She did put a cloth over my mouth, so I wouldn't inhale the fumes. She taught me how to steal and would often use my brother and me to steal food or whatever we needed.

We went all over Southern California. There was no adventure, no laughter, or family stories; there was just fear. I had my little brother now, and my focus was on him. The worst times were when mom would take us with her to shoot up. It was always in an awful place, and she would shoot up and pass out. My brother and I would sit next to her and hope she would wake up. My biggest fear was she would not wake up, and I wouldn't be able to take care of my little brother. I don't know how long it took; it was different every time. But the places were all the same: cold, dark, abandoned with nothing but the filth left behind by other users. We would sit in the filth by mom and hope she woke up.

I remember one time when I was around seven and my brother was five. We had been evicted from another apartment, so, mom took me and my little brother and put us in this broken -down car and parked it in the back of the complex parking lot out of sight. She told us not to get out for any reason. She didn't need to worry about that; we were terrified. My little brother cried non-stop and I did too when I couldn't console him, and fear overtook me. She came by once and took us to a house for an hour or two, and we had something to eat. I thought we would be ok, but, she took us back to the car. It was cold and raining, storming. My little brother and I buried ourselves under the old clothes and blankets in the back seat of the car. We dared not cry for help. I knew there was no help anyway. For the first time, I remember being really angry with mom. How could she leave us? What was going to happen to us? I wanted to be rescued and something to happen to mom, but I knew nothing would change. As the time passed and my brother's cries grew weaker. I grew weaker. I didn't think we would survive. Out of the darkness, I heard a familiar voice. It was my uncle. He was looking for mom. I took a chance and cried out. He took me and my little brother and went to find mom. When he found her, I thought he might kill her. He yelled and screamed while my little brother and I cowered in fear. During his tirade, I learned we had been in the car for four days.

BUT GOD

When addiction is mixed with poverty the results are always magnified. Addiction takes what very little money there is for necessities and uses it to feed the addiction. Most of the time there is nothing left for the children of addicts. Addiction clouds values and erodes relationships until there is no relationship left but with the drug itself. Drugs are a huge problem in poverty-stricken areas for some pretty obvious reasons. Drug dealers have access to a group of people with nothing to lose and are consequently easy to recruit to sell drugs. Addicts are easy to create when survival is a daily battle and a drug promises to take them away from their problems. Gangs take the place of families making it easy for kids to run drugs, but once these kids are in, there is no way out. Now, the big money -maker has escalated to sex trafficking. Young girls are being "sold" into this underground business in staggering numbers. They usually don't survive more than a few years before dying from disease or murder.

The poor are easy to exploit, and exploitation of the poor can be seen in politics, business, Hollywood, and even in churches. Everyone wants the "feel good" for giving to the poor or grandstanding on their behalf, but the "feel good" is, ironically, all the addict wants, too. Really helping the poor isn't about a quick fix. It is a calling and a long-term investment for which returns may not be seen for years. It requires sacrifice. Love always does.

Jesus had a lot to say about our responsibility to "the least of these." In fact, He demonstrated it over and over in the Gospels. Not once did he tell a blind man or a leper, "I will heal you if you learn how to take care of yourself first in this new program my disciples are running which will teach you how to be self-sufficient and not burden society,"; or, "when you have proven you can be trusted not to have any more "fits" or stay on your meds, I will rid you of your that demon." He didn't tell Matthew to quit collecting taxes for a living. Instead He sat down in Matthew's home for dinner, with Matthew and all his friends, and acknowledged him as a human being worth His time. No, Jesus met needs, physical and emotional, first. Then, hearts and minds were open to receive His grace and lives were changed.

Giving does make you feel good. It takes the focus from yourself and places it on another's needs. I want out ladies to have the privilege of learning how to give to one another. Our programs will all have giving to each other or someone else in the community built into them as I think giving brings joy and our women need to experience joy.

"Darkness cannot drive out darkness, only light can do that. Hate cannot drive out hate; only love can do that."

Martin Luther King, Jr.

CHAPTER 3

The first time I was "molested", that's a nice word for rape, was when I was five years old. Mom left me with my brother's grandmother's husband. She needed to go shoot up and left us on his floor playing. He was on the couch. I really hadn't noticed him. He was just another person in a long line whom mom had left us with, and we just stayed quiet and tried to disappear.
I remember him touching me and not liking it. I remember him touching my lady parts and it hurt. I remember when he penetrated my little body, and it exploded in pain. But, I was silent.

A few days later I began to bleed, and mom noticed. She told my uncle what happened. He and his friends found the pedophile and beat him within an inch of his life with a baseball bat. Then they called the police, and the pedophile got 20 years in prison for rape of a child. I wouldn't say my uncle was a good man; he did drugs too. He was decent. He did not want my brother or me hurt, and he reacted the way any addict with a conscience knows how to act and did his best to protect us.

I was in so much pain and there was so much damage to my lady parts they had to take me to the hospital. CPS removed me from my mom's care, and I was put into the foster system for the next six months. Foster care is everything you hear about. I had two sets of foster "parents," a white couple and a black couple. They both were in it for the money and had about 10-15 kids living in their home. The more kids, the bigger the paycheck. It was always chaos, yelling, screaming, beatings, but, at least I was around other children. I can even remember laughing a few times when another kid did something really silly. I learned I could meet new kids and make friends. I knew other kids lived like I did. (Really, I thought everyone lived like I did, and, this just sealed that idea for me and I knew I wasn't alone. My world was full of adults until this point.) I also learned other kids liked me, and I had a way of making them feel better.

BUT GOD

Even crime, violent crime, is viewed differently within the walls of those living in generational poverty. It goes virtually unnoticed until it spills over into mainstream society. Most people outside of poverty would rather not even look our way and are completely apathetic unless the results of poverty touch them personally. The common belief is the government and tax dollars support my community; therefore, responsibility or concern, as a tax paying citizen, should end there. At the same time, when a culture, such as people living in generational poverty, is living day to day in survival mode, in the confines of a world that distrusts, looks down on, and judges them with disdain for their existence, there appears to be no hope or even a glimpse of hope that outsiders could possibly understand their world and want to help them.

Death, Rape, Violence, Abuse, Addiction, Exploitation, Hunger, Exposure...these are landmines we face every day. Each day, beginning at birth, is a day spent dodging landmines. Crime, for the most part, in our world isn't reported. Most women and children would rather live in their known environment than be subjected to the "system" which takes all of the above landmines to a different level. At least they know what to expect at home and who the players are. In the "system" there is yet another set of rules and unknown players and sadly, the abuse often continues. Constant, smothering fear is a way of life, and fear manifests itself in anger, hatred, violence, withdrawal, depression, and poor health. Fear kills desire, creativity, and the courage to step outside our comfort zone. You cannot simply move a person in fear to a safe place. The fear has to be challenged and conquered...and that takes time.

In a way, I don't think the poor woman's pain is any different from that of a middle or upper-class woman, pain is pain. However, there are more options available for people with money. They can direct and receive care from a number of places. There are counselors, outpatient therapy, ministers, rehab and all kinds of ways to soothe their pain and try to restore their mental and spiritual health. In our world, it is survival or the system. Most opt for survival.

I know first hand how these ladies feel. I know their fear. I know how to reach them, I must meet them where they are, meet needs, and earn their trust before hearts and minds can be changed. I must commit my time and ministry to these women and remain a steady, consistent person in their lives who they can depend upon in their time of need. Trust opens the door for God's grace to come pouring in and change lives. I had the joy of watching one of our ladies give their life to Jesus one morning last year. After two years of driving her to classes and working with her in my parenting class, she called me and asked me to tell her how to become a Christian. When we prayed together the next morning, the visible change that came over her was indescribable. She is now in my discipleship class and is attending church with her children.

She like other women will come to know that Jesus sees the heart of men and women, not their checkbook, skin color, talent, or position in society. There is no sin or shame that His grace doesn't cover. All of humanity is on an equal playing field in God's eyes; we are ALL one in our need for a Savior!

"When the human race neglects its weaker members, when family neglects the weakest one; it is the first blow in a suicidal movement."

Maya Angelou

By the time I started school at seven, I had been "molested" aka raped, by two more predators: a family member and one of mom's boyfriends. Mom was in and out of prison for robbery and drug related charges, and my brother and I would be left with various people. There are too many to list, and I really don't remember any names or places anyway. They are all a clip from the same bad dream. I never settled anywhere and had no idea what it was like to have my own bed, a bathroom, or a hot shower. There were no bedtime stories or bedtime routines. We dropped and slept wherever Mom took us. We went through the day as invisible by-standers in her world and even more invisible in the darkness. We never stayed anywhere long, and we never had money for rent or to live anywhere; so, we house- jumped, slept in cars, abandoned buildings, or on the streets.

School was a nightmare. I was bullied all the time. My clothes were dirty, I was dirty, my hair was never combed, I ate more than the other kids. They didn't know I wouldn't eat again until I came back to school the next day. I wasn't able to make friends. I mean, where would I take them for a "play date", really. I would go home to beatings, violence, rape, and my little body withstood it all. But the constant mean, cruel words of my classmates hurt in places I had never known before. It hurt in places band-aids or hospitals couldn't fix. The words became just as impactful as the blows of a hit. The bruises on my body were nothing compared to the bruises to my soul. I was now living in constant fear not only of the adults in my world but also children.

I did discover in the midst of it all, I loved to learn. I could escape in learning. I could learn for me. When I would go to a school I would find a place to hide and read. It filled my mind with a world outside of my own. Learning gave me hope.

BUT GOD

Every woman I work with today has been sexually abused or raped as children or as a teenager. Every woman I disciple has lived in fear and shame most of her life. We have been living like this for generations, and yet no one has wanted to help us. We have been used and abused in horrific ways and it never makes national news. I want to scream when I hear all the stories out of Hollywood! This is nothing new. We have been crying for years only to fall on deaf ears. Yet another reason for our community to believe we don't matter to anyone.

Our women's children are faced with the same fears they face which only adds to their existing anxiety. They, like most mothers, want their children to be safe. They want to feed and clothe them, and they want them to be good people. They just don't have a roadmap, example, or mentor to show them the way.

I think this is a good place to shed some light on what these women face and the choices they make each day living in generational poverty.

A single woman with 2-3 children on welfare has housing provided by the government and receives food stamps. Well, that covers it, right? Let's talk about the housing first.

Good, safe housing is hard to come by and is always full. To get into an existing government home (apartment), someone will need to be kicked out, move out (which rarely happens) or die. *If you are single with no children, you have no chance.* If you have one child, you move up on the list and so on. So, yes, our system is designed to reward having children.

If government housing isn't available, then there are the slumlords. These human beings are the equal to tax collectors in the Bible. They prey on their own people and extort and humiliate them for their own personal gain. Upkeep on their rental homes is a joke,and they use fear to keep their tenants in line. If the heating breaks in the middle of January, it might get fixed by the next year (more often, never.) That is when you go into homes and they are being heated by keeping the oven door open, or worse, by cheap space heaters which often catch fire. Likewise, there is no air conditioning in summer. Bugs are everywhere ranging from roaches to termites, not to mention rats and mice. If the plumbing is out, you are at the mercy of the slumlord. It might get fixed in a few weeks. Rent is often 3 X what it should be; therefore, you have multiple families under one roof to afford a roof over your head. This leads to a whole lot of other problems. Some, like mom and me, moved from house to house. We had places to "stay" but never a home. People would let us "crash" on their floor for the night. We had no possessions to speak of, only what we could carry or fit in the trunk of a car.

For the most part, the government housing is clean and nice; but, once you have the roof over your head, assistance stops there. You still pay rent; you still have to pay to have things fixed (leaky sinks, toilets, air filters – this is required and cost $50 to change 2X per year, and so on). Most women have tried to work, but, if a child is sick, there is no support system to provide care, so, she misses work. If the woman has a car, it usually isn't a good one and is in constant need of repair...which she cannot afford, so public transportation (which costs money) is her only option. Also, if a woman has been convicted of certain crimes, which many women have, they are not eligible for government housing and their only option is dealing with slumlords, moving in with other people, living on the streets, or shelters.

There is only one bus stop in South Dallas, Bonton neighborhood, where I live. It can take hours to go to and from work depending on bus routes. If she misses the bus, she misses work. For these reasons, most women cannot hold a job. After three or four times being fired for attendance (which you cannot blame the business owners), she succumbs to taking only government assistance and what it can provide.

If she chooses to leave children at home alone or in the care of her other children to go to work, they are wide open for predators. Or, if they dodge that landmine, she gets caught, and protective services will take them and they are put into the system (for a different kind of predator). So, there really is no choice.

Now for food stamps. Food stamps cover food. They do not cover, paper products, cleaning supplies, feminine products, soap and other toiletries, diapers, etc. To get those things, she must make a choice. She must sell a portion of her food stamps in exchange for the money to purchase these items. Also, remember the one bus? Try taking the bus to a grocery store sometime. If it is crowded, the most you can carry is two bags. Also, you must walk a few blocks from the bus stop to the store. Just that eliminates purchasing any frozen foods and, in the summer, any food that can spoil. The average trip to the store takes about three hours. However, there are lots of liquor stores and convenience stores in the neighborhood. At night, all the dealers are out front ready to prey on you and your children. The prices are inflated due to their "captive" shopper (usually owned and operated by the same slumlords who exploit housing).

We don't have bank accounts or budgets. When a person is surviving like this; budgets go out the window. There is a negative balance on paper each month and no way to build any kind of savings. This is just a glimpse of the daily obstacles women face in poverty.

We what we do see routinely is an abundance of is JUDGMENT.

There was a lot of Judgement going around in Jesus' day especially among the religious leaders who were constantly judging and pointing fingers at the poor, the sick, and the least of these. Jesus, on the other hand, was constantly pointing out the humility and worthiness of His love for the poor, the sick, and the least of these. This never went over too well with the rich, the educated, and the righteous. It is no mistake that God sent His Son to be born to a poor, humble family, in a manger at that. It is no mistake that the first people to see Jesus were shepherds, who were the lowest of the low when Jesus came into our world.

This alone should be enough for any Christian to set aside judgment of the poor and quit pointing fingers, but rather, extend the hand of grace and mercy that God has extended to them and meet and love the poor where they are. Not all are called to hands-on ministry; but, we are all called to help those who are.

"I have learned now that while those who speak about one's miseries usually hurt, those who keep silence, hurt more."

CS Lewis

CHAPTER 5

When I was nine, I had an accident on the playground. I hurt my left leg and it wouldn't get better. It was swollen and painful. Finally, the school got in touch with mom and told her I needed to go to a hospital. She had my grandmother take me. The doctors did a biopsy and told my grandmother I had a rare cancer. They told her I had about a 3% chance of survival and that they needed to do surgery right away followed by chemotherapy and radiation. I had the surgery and then started the chemotherapy and radiation as an outpatient. I got so sick. I threw up all the time, lost weight, lost my hair...I wanted to die. There was no one there to comfort me or encourage me. In fact, I was an inconvenience.

I had no idea how serious my cancer was, and I didn't know what all the treatments were for either. It was just more suffering and I was used to pain. I really didn't know what it meant to die; I just knew if you died it meant you did not have to deal with life anymore. In that way dying sounded appealing, but, I felt this need to live and protect my little brother. So, as best I knew how, I fought to live.

Mom was never able to do anything for long. She quit taking me for my chemo and radiation treatments. Then, when I was about 10, she was arrested again and was put in prison. I went back into the CPS system, but this time, my aunt petitioned for custody and won, and I went to live with her. She took me back for a follow up appointment with the doctor, and because I had not finished treatment, the cancer had recurred and become very aggressive. The doctor told them their hospital was not able to treat this cancer, and I would need to get care in a place that specialized in childhood cancer.

My aunt and my grandmother went to visit Mom in jail, and they agreed the best thing to do was take me back to Dallas to be with my dad and seek medical care in Dallas. I was brought back to Dallas to live with my dad. At this point in my life, I thought my dad was my best friend. He was kind to me and he seemed to care about me. He had even come out to California to visit and make sure I was ok a few times. Those were the only good memories of California I had. The problem with my dad was he just loved to drink more than he liked being a dad, so, in my young mind, he was just a friend. The first thing he did when I returned to Dallas was regain custody and change my last name from Simpson to Thomas.

BUT GOD

If anyone has ever had a sick child, life is temporarily put on hold to care for your sick child. There are pediatrician visits followed by medicine and a plan to get well. Taking a child to the doctor is problematic for the poor. Chances are, if you do have a job, you will need to miss work to take your child to the doctor. Doctor's visits are not an hour or two- hour event. They take all day long. There is no money, so, free medical care is the only option. If you want to keep your job, the ER is the only other option. The children cannot go to school sick, so, they either stay home all day by themselves, or the older children stay home with them, or, mom stays home and loses her job. Then, medicine. That takes about as long to get as seeing the doctor. The instructions for dosing are impossible to follow sometimes; so, the mother improvises. (i.e. take 3 times a day with food. Well, we don't eat 3 meals a day; so, I will give all 3 pills at one time with the 1 meal we do eat; or, I'll just give one pill when we eat...) Everything is complicated. There is nothing simple in our world.

I had cancer. My mom was in no way equipped to care for a terminally ill child. We were living on the streets! My mom never knew from one day to the next where we would be living and a child throwing up with constant diarrhea from chemotherapy didn't allow many people to open their living space to our little family. She was out trying to score drugs or sell drugs for money all day, and at night, she would walk the streets with us or crash with anyone who would take us. It was bad enough with two babies; now she had a sick one. Keeping appointments were a joke. No one intervened and tried to help. Not a single social worker was notified when I missed life- saving treatment. I just drifted back into the darkness, and no one cared. That is what it is like being a "statistic." This is what it is like for women and children living in generational poverty. This is why it is not news to us to hear about a mentally ill women escorted out of a hospital in the wee hours of the morning, naked (or nearly naked) in sub-zero temperature and left at bus stop to fend for herself. Our only surprise was it made the news.

In the Bible, people who were sick were simply put out of the cities and towns. It was necessary to prevent the spread of disease, but, they bore the shame of being an outcast on top of their disease. The mentally ill were in the same boat. No one knew how to handle men or women possessed by demons, or with any uncontrollable physical or mental problem. They just tossed them out to survive. They were "dead" to family and society at that point. What is interesting is the rich, the poor, Jew, or Gentile; illness made you an equal. If you found yourself with a known disease like leprosy, you became a "leper" and were put out of the city. You were no longer a mother, father, carpenter, scribe, Pharisee, soldier, tax collector...you were a leper and that was your only identity.

Again, it is no mistake that we see Jesus over and over in scripture meeting these people where they are. He seeks them and finds them in their pain. He touches them when most had not felt a human touch in years. Not only were His disciples amazed; the sick were too. They had accepted their place in society and had no hope at all of ever being made whole or accepted in the world ever again. Then Jesus meets them and not only restores their health but also their dignity...though personal interaction and touch. He found them worthy of His grace. He found them worthy of mercy.

Jesus demonstrates the need to break down the walls of class and division over and over in His ministry. He clearly shreds any argument one might have for prejudice or self-righteousness in the parable of the Good Samaritan (Luke 10: 25-37) when He answers the question, "who is our neighbor?" There is no better parable for our world today.

The women I serve are not just my neighbors; they are yours too. They need healing and restoration. They need their dignity restored.   They need Jesus. They need you.

"What does love look like? It has the hands to help others. It has the feet to hasten to the poor and needy. It has eyes to see misery and want. It has ears to hear the sighs and sounds of men. That is what love looks like."

St. Augustine.

CHAPTER 6

I will never forget walking into Children's Hospital in Dallas. There was this train that went all the way around the room and it looked so real. I loved the sound it made, and I could stand with the other kids and watch it for hours. There were little towns and bridges, and the train would move through them on the tracks and go up and down hills and around curves with ease. It was the most beautiful thing I had ever seen. To this day, I love trains, and riding on one is on my bucket list!

The first time I was admitted to Children's Hospital, I was in a room by myself. My dad did come and visit and stay a couple of nights, but, it was too hard for him. My grandmother would come visit and she would pray over me. That's the first time I can remember hearing the name of Jesus and hearing a prayer. I had no idea what it meant, but, it brought peace and I needed peace in my little life. I had a roof over my head, a hot meal, a bed to sleep in, a shower; things that I had never had in my entire life, at least not on a consistent basis.

The treatment started and it was awful. After some time, they let me have outpatient treatment, and I would go back and forth from my dad's house to the hospital. I had endured a lot worse and to me, for a time, in spite of my cancer, I had peace.

Eventually, the cancer was too aggressive for outpatient treatment, and I was re-admitted to the hospital. This time, I had a roommate and we hit it off immediately. Cancer is not prejudiced. It strikes the good, the bad, the rich, the poor, and race makes no difference. She was my first friend and my best friend...and she was white. We talked about our cancer, our feelings, what we liked and didn't like. We laughed a lot. I had never laughed so much in my life. We laughed because we were both so skinny and bald; we made up crazy names for ourselves, the nurses, and mimicked all the hospital staff. We would laugh until we got sick! We became very close and I loved her so much.

She couldn't get around as well as I could; so I would sneak out of the room and go up and down the halls to make sure the coast was clear. Then I would go back and tell her the lay of the land. She would put her mask on and we would sneak up and down the hallways and giggle and laugh. It was a great adventure!

She had lots of visitors, which meant I did too! Her mom would talk to me as much as she would her daughter. My friend was allergic to chocolate, but, her mom made me chocolate chip cookies and I had never had one. It was the best thing I had ever tasted. I had never had a Christmas present and I didn't know who Santa was, but, for Christmas, her mom gave me a sweatshirt that said, "Be Naughty, Save Santa the Trip!" I wore it until it was thread bare.

I was the happiest I had ever been in my whole life. I saw a real family for the first time and I fit in. They prayed for me and the nurses prayed for me. I was loved, and I had never felt that kind of love before and really didn't have a name for it, so, I named it" peace."

One day I came back from radiation and they wouldn't let me go back to my room. They took me to a room down the hall. No one would tell me why and all I wanted to do was get in my bed and laugh and talk to my friend. I had a great new impression of one of the hospital staff members and couldn't wait to show her. I knew she would fall out laughing.

A little while later, her mom came into my room. She was crying. I was confused. She put her arms around me and told me my friend had died. I couldn't believe it. Children don't die. We weren't that sick. But when it finally sank in and I understood I would never see her again, all the chemo and radiation in the world couldn't touch the pain I felt. The tears wouldn't stop and my anger grew. My best friend in the whole world was gone. God took my only friend. Why? Was I next?

The nurses at Children's Hospital are the best in the world. They talked to me all the time about my loss and how I felt. They prayed for me and with me, but, I still didn't understand. Even though I had no idea who God was or even what love was, the prayers comforted me. If they believed in a God who would be with me, then that was fine with me. I didn't know if I would ever have another friend or if I would ever laugh again. But, somehow, I found a way to push through and I survived a bone cancer that only 3% of the people in the world survive. I didn't know why. What made me survive when my friend did not? I was so angry and scared.

BUT GOD

People living in generational poverty live with daily loss, but, it doesn't mean that we don't have feelings like everyone else. We just build a lot of walls to stay "tough" to survive our daily landmines and keep pushing forward. The tenacity to live, to survive is a strong force so you can only imagine that the walls placed to defend it are solid and almost impenetrable. Women, who are so often the most vulnerable and have suffered the most, have very little trust for anyone. Even though my neighborhood is full of women going through the same problems, each little family unit remains isolated because isolation means safe in our world.

This is why the cycle of generational poverty is so difficult to break. There is no way to reach our women until a relationship of trust is built, and that takes a lot of time and a lot of patience. Working with women with this level of pain requires understanding that change will only take place in very small steps and there are no shortcuts. Time is the investment needed, a lot of it. Real and lasting change will occur when we learn to trust each other and support each other, when we come together in our suffering and heal together within our own communities. Change will come from the inside out, not by outside forces. We need to raise Godly leaders from among us who will commit to bringing about renewal and restoration.

The early Christians were all about community. They had joy overflowing because they were unified and trusted each other in a world that was in constant opposition to them and in spite of the fact they were always at high risk for persecution. In Acts 10: 9-48 God makes it clear to Peter that he is "not to call any person common or unclean," and Peter later proclaims, "Truly, I understand that God shows no partiality, but in every nation, anyone who fears Him and does what is right is acceptable to Him…" After this declaration, there was an outpouring of the Holy Spirit and lives were changed.

People are not going to be changed by programs, friends. They will be changed by love. They will be changed when they meet Jesus shining through us.

"No pit is so deep that He is not deeper still."

Corrie Ten Boom

CHAPTER 7

I left the hospital cancer free. I moved in with my dad, his wife, and her two boys. She was pregnant with her third son. She was a nurse and worked two jobs and was never home. She took care of my dad's needs. She would bathe him and help him dress each day, things that the palsy wouldn't allow him to do on his own. My dad was terribly abusive, verbally, to her. Sometimes I wondered why he was so mean to her when she was helping him. By that time, I had seen so much abuse, it seemed normal. What wasn't normal was, in spite of his nasty temper and pure meanness, she still cared for him.

I had to be home schooled at first because of my cancer, which meant I was at home all the time. It wasn't long before I could see my dad look at me differently. I not only was taking care of myself but also him and my little step brothers as well. It started with his asking me to come sit on his lap or come lay next to him in the bed. Soon it escalated to his wanting to kiss me. His wife noticed, and it made her angry at me. I wanted to scream to the top of my lungs that I had not done anything and I hated what he did, but, I didn't know how or what to say. I was barely 11 years old. That year for Christmas her boys all received Christmas gifts but I did not. She felt my dad had chosen me over her. My dad didn't even acknowledge Christmas much less give me a gift. That was my first Christmas.

BUT GOD

Other than the Christmas gift given to me by my friend's mother, I had never celebrated Christmas before. I really had no idea what it was and it was very confusing. All of a sudden people would descend on our neighborhood out of nowhere and give the kids toys for Christmas. Even then, I didn't receive anything. People would get food; my family didn't get any. All of that must have been for other people and I had no idea how they got it. And Santa, really? If I am a good girl, I would get presents Christmas morning? Really? I wasn't going to hold my breath on that one. Jesus was never mentioned in association with any of this, or, if He was, I don't remember. It was a complete surprise to me, later, when I learned that Christmas was actually a celebration of Jesus' birth and had nothing to do with Santa and toys.

A parent has to fill out a form or get on a list for their children to receive gifts. Addicts and many of my neighbors don't care too much for forms. If you have ever tried to fill out any kind of form for assistance, especially government assistance, you practically need a PHD, and any visit to seek government assistance is an all day affair. Sometimes the questions on the forms can be answered 100 different ways, depending on your interpretation of them, and that is assuming the person can read. For example: what is your household income? Well, does that mean government assistance I already have? Does it mean my baby daddy (who doesn't live with me and rarely gives me money); my teenager works and makes a few dollars a week...does that count? We want to give the right answer and even an honest one, but, what do they want? If you answer it wrong, you are out. There are forms for everything. We will be teaching our women how to fill out forms. We will also teach how to apply for driver's licenses, to get birth certificates, shot records, and all the different documents we need to enroll our children in school and for them to seek employment.

I am still not much on giving gifts at Christmas. I like to give year-round. I like birthdays. That is the day we try to make our women feel special. I want to let them know the day they came into this world was no accident and they are special. We celebrate their life and hopefully give them a day to be happy about their life and validate them and love on them. I do the same thing with Jesus at Christmas. That's HIS birthday. So, Kevin and I give to Him that day. We want Him to know how thankful we are He came into our world and the joy He brings to all who receive Him.

"I don't know what kind of courage it took thousands of years ago, but I know how courageous women need to be today."

Beth Moore

CHAPTER 8

I had just survived a two-year battle with bone cancer at age 11. I had lost my best friend. I was with my dad, who I thought, was my friend. Once again, though, I was in Hell and there was no way out for me. There wasn't even a different life I could even dream about. I was trapped forever, and my abused, frail body was at the mercy of a sick, depraved man who this time, was my own father.

One day I was in the boys' room and he came in, told the boys to leave, and locked the door. He kissed my breasts and put his hands all over my body. I cried. He performed oral sex on me and forced me to do the same to him. And, finally he moved on to penetrating me. He raped me over and over, almost every day. I couldn't tell anyone. I was a child. Alone, sick, hurting and no one cared! Who would I tell? He blamed alcohol, he blamed his wife for not loving him and making him feel like a man, he blamed me. He knew what he was doing was wrong, but, he enjoyed it. I would cry and he would be enjoying himself. I did not understand it. I still don't. I don't think I ever will.

I went back to school, and that at least gave me some time out of the house. I made friends with a girl who had a "normal" life. She had parents who were married to each other and had a good marriage. I loved going over to her house. One night, when I was around 13, my dad tried to rape me again. This time I ran. I ran to my friend's house and told them what my father had done to me. The police came, and he lied. He told them I was a runaway making things up to stay out of trouble. The police left. That night my dad beat me so hard and so long with an extension cord that I could not go to school for a week because of the pain and the visible whelps all over my body. He all but killed me.

Not long after that he tried to rape me again. This time I found his gun and held it to his head and pulled the trigger. If the gun had fired, my life would have been ruined. He called the police, and they put me in handcuffs while he watched. When he decided not to press charges, I paid for it with sex.

BUT GOD

There are no words to describe sexual assault. I had been assaulted multiple times before but at the hands of my father...there was nowhere to put that in my mind. I could not escape it. I did exactly what I should have done. I trusted an adult to help me, and, praise God, they tried. But, the reality is, our systems, by design, are built to distrust the victim and protect the guilty; especially women and children. The police never questioned my father. They didn't even suggest a social worker come by for a home visit. Instead, they turned me back over to my abuser which almost cost me my life. It has taken me years to overcome my distrust of law enforcement. I am not alone. In defense of our police officers, there is so much violent crime every day that they really cannot handle each one. But women and children are the ones who pay the price in generational poverty. Women in my ministry live or have lived with so much abuse at the hands of so many only to face the daily struggle to provide for themselves and children; any other life seems like a fairy tale. They accept their position in life in order to survive. But, we all have a breaking point and as in my case, if my father had chosen to prosecute, I would have gone to prison. All the abuse that led to that moment would have had no weight in deciding my fate in a court of law. That is the reality today for women unless they are lucky and can afford an awesome lawyer. Public defenders rarely look into the history or try to get help for women charged with crimes. I think some of that may be because the women are so shut down and hardened when they meet with the attorney, since there is zero trust that this person can help them, they stay quiet. They also know that whatever "crime" they committed will not only bring punishment from the law but also when they return to their community. Their children will go into the system ("to protect them") and the fight will begin to regain custody of them. They will come back damaged and disillusioned and they have now witnessed first- hand how the system works.

I thank God to this day that the gun did not fire. I would be in jail for life or on death row for murder had the gun fired. To this day, I believe God stopped that bullet from leaving the chamber of that gun; it was a miracle.

When men brought the woman caught in adultery to Jesus, I have always wondered what he wrote in the sand. In fact, in John's gospel, there are two encounters with women who were sleeping around or even may have been victims themselves. We see the Samaritan woman in chapter 4 and then in chapter 8 the woman caught in adultery. In both stories, the woman was an outcast and was used by men for sexual pleasure. The men involved are not part of the story. Jesus makes a point to bring restoration to each woman, to defend and show mercy to these two women. Jesus knew the whole story. He knew all of the players. He knew their position in the world. So what does He do? He elevates these women to an equal position with men in terms of grace... a pretty radical move in those days.

"Teacher, this woman has been caught in adultery" ...Jesus bent down and wrote with His finger on the ground. And as they continued to ask Him (about the law to stone her), He stood up and said to them, "Let him who without sin among you be the first to throw a stone at her." And once more he bent down and wrote on the ground. But when they heard it, they went away one by one...and Jesus was left alone with the woman standing before Him. "Woman, where are they? Has no one condemned you?" She said, "No one, Lord." And Jesus said, "Neither do I condemn you; go, and from now on sin no more." (John 8:1-11)

I like to think, sometimes, that maybe he wrote the names of the men involved. Adultery was punishable by Jewish law, even for men (not to the extent of women.) Maybe he wrote the law on adultery which would have shed light on their own sin...John left that part out on purpose, I think. But if ever women doubt their importance to Jesus, read the Gospels. Women are listed with the disciples. Mary Magdalene is the first to see the risen Christ. Mary and Martha are friends with Jesus. The gospels validate women and their worth to Jesus. And if we are valued by the God of the universe and we know Him, then we can begin to love ourselves as the first step in healing. This is the gospel our women need to hear!

"The world is a dangerous place, not because of those who do evil, but because of those who do nothing."

Albert Einstein

CHAPTER 9

When I went back to school, I met a boy in my class that I really liked. We quickly became sexually active. It wasn't long before I got pregnant. I was 14 years old and in 8th grade. I continued to go to school every day. I was very small, and no one could tell I was pregnant. I received no prenatal care or counseling. I had no idea what was going on in my own body. The baby kicked me one night and it nearly scared me to death. I was alone, scared, and angry. I had no idea what to do or what to expect.

I was in class one day in May when my water broke. The teacher about fell out. She asked me if I was pregnant and when I told her I was, she called 911. I was taken to Parkland Hospital, and Archesicia Raychelle Thomas was born into the world. My dad and his lady friend were with me when she was born. I was 5 ½ months pregnant when I went into labor. I only saw my daughter for a minute before she was rushed to the neonatal ICU. My only words when I saw her were, "I don't want this." She remained in ICU for two weeks. She weighted 4lbs 2 oz,. and her head was very large in comparison to her body. I started calling her "Tweety" (after Tweety Bird in the cartoons) and it has stuck ever since. Kind of like "Chocolate" for me. By now, my mom had several more children who were all bi-racial. Since I was the only "pure black" sibling and my skin was dark, she and all her family started referring to me as the "chocolate" baby. Pretty soon, that is all they called me. It wasn't meant to be nice at all at and at the time, it really hurt.

In spite of what I said, I would catch the bus every day and go see her. I had no idea what to do with her or how we would survive. If I had known about adoption, I would have given her to a family that could love her and take care of her. Since I didn't, I promised myself she would not have the same life I lived. She would not be homeless, hungry, or abused. I was back living with my dad because my boyfriend's family didn't want me there. I would constantly lie in bed, with Tweety beside me and try to come up with a plan for us. I had no idea what to do or how to take care of us, but, I was determined to try. The only good thing at that point in my life was with Tweety in my bed, my dad left me alone.

BUT GOD

As a rule, in the world of people living in generational poverty, sex has nothing to do with love. We see sex acted out in front of us from the time we are small children. That is what happens when multiple "family units" are living in small quarters. We see both healthy and unhealthy sex. We see sex by force, sex by consent, violent sex, and sex between the old and young. It is very visual and unhidden. The lack of privacy and intimacy further distances the concept of love and sex going together. Mainstream media inundates our culture with sex, and the more this happens, I think, the more numbed we will all be to love and intimacy. What a loss.

Just like the sex act, the consequences are common and a way of life. Teenage pregnancy is nothing to be ashamed of. STD's and AIDS are common. We see the results, but given the frequency sex is forced on women (children), there is little that can be done to prevent the spread of disease.

Marriage is the exception not the rule. The concept of a man and women living together in unity, for life, is virtually never seen; therefore, children have no model to follow. They have no clue why anyone would want to marry. If they look outside their own world, they see how sex is portrayed in the media. They see women having multiple big, expensive weddings they cannot possibly fathom. Women are not getting married but very publically moving from man to man (and each relationship is headlined the "love of their life," "their soulmate", etc.), and now same sex marriage. No wonder they have no clue what the connection between love, sex, and marriage might be. The irony of it all is the sex act itself was supposed to be one of the most precious gifts God gave us; yet, our society has reduced it to the ranks of brushing your teeth. (If you don't believe me, look at toothpaste and mouthwash ads!) It is also ironical that today, a person's sexual identity is more important than her mind, spirituality, or accomplishments. Who you are as a person is first identified by sexual preference, and all the other things about a person follow in rank. Therefore, outsiders are hardened to the reality our women live in every day and judge them as if this is all their choice and they somehow deserve the consequences of their choices just like anyone else. It gets really crude, too. "We should make them all get their tubes tied." "If they would quit having all those babies, they could help themselves." "People try to help but they won't help themselves." "They have the same opportunity as everyone else in America." and my favorite, "They don't even love their children; look how they live."

God's light and truth are greater than any of the lies Satan tells us. In my community, we are seeing more and more women wanting something different in their lives. They are looking to God for a model and not mainstream media. I have already married one couple in my ministry. The woman wanted commitment in her life. She wanted to be valued and cherished as someone's wife. God's model was the best model she could find, and she and her husband wanted that for their relationship. We married another couple not long after that. Women in my community see God's perfect plan in contrast to the destructive relationships around them, and that is creating a desire to follow God's plan. His light is penetrating our world. It is very exciting to see, and I believe this is the beginning of our community turning around.

The Bible is full of love stories. It is full of examples of men loving women and cherishing them. It is full of genuine love for their spouse. We really don't need to look further than Joseph. Now, Joseph could have done any number of thing when he found out that his fiancé, Mary, was pregnant, and not by him. He could have sought the advice of his friends, exposing Mary. He could have had her stoned. But, even before the angel speaks to him in a dream, he has already decided to protect her. After the angel departs, he is obedient to God. But Joseph doesn't just treat Mary like an obligation. He takes her to Bethlehem with him to make sure she was safe and to be sure that no self-righteous busy body harmed her or the baby that was conceived "out of wedlock" while he was in Bethlehem. In fact, he goes to great lengths to protect her and the child even after they are married. He moves to a different county to raise him! There are acts of love, not obligation. This is a model for men today on how to treat, treasure, and love their wife. Jesus' parents speak volumes to us today and give us a real, non-scripted, non-Hollywood inspired look at love, trust, commitment, and unity.   I married a man like Joseph who loves me and cares for me from his heart for God and for me.

"The hunger for love is much more difficult to remove than the hunger for bread."

Mother Teresa

CHAPTER 10

My dad was a mess. I don't know why. He didn't want me around any more. When Tweety was two months old, Dad put me on a bus to California at midnight one night. He packed me and Tweety up and took us to the bus station and left us there. He lied and said my mom had OD'd and was dying. He told my grandmother in California I was an unruly teenager. He didn't tell her about the baby. It turns out Mom wasn't dying at all. She was back in jail. He put me on that bus and sent me away in the middle of the night to the pits of Hell. I wanted to die. I wanted to kill myself. I wanted it all to go away.

I got in touch with my cousin who came to pick us up. I couldn't find my grandmother. My cousin couldn't support me and Tweety as she had four kids of her own. Somehow, she pulled together enough money for a plane ticket and sent us back to Dallas. It was my first time on a plane, and it was the only bright thing I remember. It was so beautiful and peaceful in the clouds. Tweety was in my arms, and it was just the two of us. We were flying above the pain and abuse; no one could touch us. I didn't want to be a mom. I had taken care of children my whole life. I had never had a childhood. Yet, here this little baby was in my arms, and she was depending on me. This little baby turned out to be the gift from God that changed my life.

BUT GOD

Suicide is almost unheard of in my community. In a way we are so busy trying to stay alive; we don't think about dying. We die, alright, early, either from violence or disease. I thought about dying a lot. I was 14 years old and I felt like I was 100. The physical, emotional, and mental abuse I had survived had left me drained of life with no desire to move on. This little life I held in my arms was the only reason for living. I only wanted to be sure she was not born into the world I lived in, and it was up to me to prevent that from happening but, I was only 14.

I think this is one reason I can relate to another Joseph in the Bible. The one whose brothers sold him into slavery. He was probably about my age when that happened. He was alone, in a foreign country and had no idea what his future held. He was accused and thrown into prison (I just went to the pits of Hell in California) and there was no apparent advocate or justice to be found. But God had this master plan. A plan to use all the terrible things that he endured and use them to create a leader like Egypt had never seen before. And when he had the chance for revenge, he gave mercy.

"Do not fear, for am I in the place of God? As for you, you meant evil against me, but God meant it for good, to bring it about that many people should be kept alive, as they are today. " (Genesis 50:21)

Later, Jesus gives us a prayer for forgiveness..."Forgive us our sins as we forgive those who have sinned against us." (Matthew 6:12)

This is why I can forgive my mother, my rapists, my father, and all the others who hurt me through neglect or turning a blind eye...what they meant as evil, God has used to build me into the woman I am today.

"You might be poor, your shoes might be broken, but your mind is a palace."

Frank McCourt
from "Angela's Ashes

CHAPTER 11

Tweety and I moved in with my grandmother and grandfather. Tweety was now 6 months old and oh how she captured the hearts of her grandparents. I asked my friend's parents to be her godparents, and they had her christened in their church. Because they always wanted to babysit her, there was an ongoing battle between my grandparents and her godparents for "Tweety time." This worked out great for me.

The Dallas schools offered amazing programs for teen mothers. I took advantage of everything they offered. For the first time in my life I was surrounded by positive people, mentors and counselors who wanted me to be successful and were there to help me when I needed help. People who poured into me to build me up from the inside so I could overcome the past and have a future. People helped with my daughter. My grandmother took me to church. Boy, did we ever go to church. If the doors were open, we were there! It started to sink in that there was a God who loved me and wanted good things for me. I wasn't sure about it all, but, God caught my attention through the constant pouring into me by my grandmother. God was building a support system for me, and I didn't even know it.

I would take Tweety to school with me and leave her in the day care while I was in class. They offered parenting education, psychological counseling, a diaper program, and a mentorship program. I was determined to get through high-school, so I could earn money to take care of us.

At home, my grandmother was always pouring into me how much God loved me, to forgive all those who had wronged me, and she knew, she was adamant, I was called to be something special. I had never had anyone think of me as special and I certainly had never had so many people in my life trying to help me and asking nothing in return. I was beginning to believe there was a Higher Power I could learn to trust and started to believe God really might be real.

BUT GOD

All the programs out there are wonderful tools if you are able to take advantage of them. I had a support system. Without that support system, I would have missed school, not had the enrichment programs that helped so much, and probably would have never made it through high-school. Support is everything. It is why so many programs fail. If they require getting in the car or bus and leaving the neighborhood, attendance will not be consistent. It can't be. There are too many things to rely on to get them there. Women who are abused are fearful and uncomfortable in strange places. It is critical that help comes to them where they are. This is true for all programs whether they are medical, educational, or spiritual. We need to connect with our neighbors and build community...build a support system. Boots on the ground. Not a once or twice a week program, not a class, not education (even those are all good), but a

24-7 support system to be there ready to help and support whatever the need may be. I know this can be built in my community, and I know the impact it will have. People ask me all the time how I made it out of poverty and most cannot. Support. One small word with powerful meaning and results.

Jesus met people where they were all the time. He traveled all over Israel. The early churches were all about community and supporting each other. Paul talks about unity within the church body all the time as well as loving and supporting each other. It wasn't a once a week on Sunday relationship in their church body. Unity was critical to the spread of Christianity. The sense of community outsiders witnessed, the love they saw among believers for each other, and the support...this is what drew people to Jesus. In a cold, violent world Christians were a shining light because of their community and their love and support for each other. So, why wouldn't that be true today? Times really haven't changed that much from the times these Christians lived. We are a violent, cold world in need of a Savior. But when the world looks on our lives as Christians, do they want to join in? Are our churches a light where people of all walks of life feel welcome and nurtured? As a great preacher once said, "Our churches should be a hospital for sinners rather than a haven for saints." Do people wonder what is different about us, or do we look like every other group? Do they see unity, genuine love, and support for each other? If not, that's a real problem.

I am going out on a limb here. But if all the churches in this country committed themselves to serving their neighbors like these early churches, I bet we wouldn't even need government programs. Just sayin'.

" *The will of God will not take us where the grace of God cannot sustain us.*"

Billy Graham

CHAPTER 12

I got a driver's license at 16 so I could attend night classes. I went to summer school as well. I graduated from high-school in 1999, a full year ahead of schedule. Things were moving forward, and the past was being pushed more and more out of my mind.

Then, my grandmother died. Tweety was two years old. This was the worst loss of my life. She had become my greatest cheerleader, my champion, my light. She had loved me well, and all the pain and darkness had been replaced with good things in her home. She taught me about forgiveness. She told me I needed to do two things to overcome the pain and hurt in my life, "forgive and forgive again..." My grandmother introduced me to Jesus. I was devastated.

At this point, I knew I could not live with anyone else. I was not going to risk being dependent on anyone out of fear for myself and Tweety. I got my first apartment when I was 17. I lied on the application and the apartments didn't perform a background check. It was a two-bedroom, one bath apartment in West Dallas. I had very little income but I had a roof over our heads. My apartment was kept clean and I could provide food. We slept on a mattress on the tile floor for the first six months and had no furniture. It was enough. Later, my aunt gave me a bed for Tweety and me to sleep in. As time passed, others gave us a love seat and more furniture. My mentor gave Tweety a fancy white bedroom suite. She was so excited about it!

I had been working at Burger King for the last year and half. I left that job to work for Weiner's Shoe Store. I only worked there for about six months and then landed a job with the YMCA working in the day care. There were two really great things about working for the YMCA. I received free day care for Tweety while I worked; and, they offered a paid education. I knew that education was my ticket to a better life for Tweety and me. But I was impatient.

I married at 18. I had maintained a relationship with a boy from high school. He had gone to college but was kicked out for selling weed. We started dating not long after he came back to the neighborhood and when he asked me to marry him, I said yes. Our wedding was held in my apartment, and my friend's father officiated the ceremony. We wore blue jeans and matching plaid shirts and Nikes. He moved into my apartment but the stability and life I hoped he would bring to Tweety (now almost 4) and me didn't last long. It started with verbal abuse and quickly escalated to a slap, then, hard hit or push, and finally to a beating.

He never laid a hand on Tweety. He loved her. He always waited for her to be staying with her god-parents for the really bad beatings (which was often) and was careful not to let her see his meanness.

At first, I thought it was worth it. After all, we were a "family." He never touched Tweety and she loved him. I wasn't moving around from place to place, and, we had things, things I had never had growing up. I had accomplished my goals to provide and then some. So, in my mind, I justified the beatings and stayed.

BUT GOD

That verse in the Bible about being "submissive" to your husband is one of the most misrepresented verses in the Bible. "Wives, submit to your own husbands, as to the Lord. For the husband is the head of the wife even as Christ is the head of the church, his body, and is himself its Savior. Now, as the church submits to Christ, so also wives should submit in everything to their husband." (Ephesians 5: 22-24.) These verses are often used as part of the "Wife-Beater's Handbook." I went to a conference a few years ago in which the speaker spoke exclusively about spiritual abuse and how that verse was used over and over by women to justify being beaten to a pulp by the "spiritual head" of the family.

Being beaten happens every day in my community. One women I know has been put in the hospital at least three or four times at the hands of her boyfriend. He is on drugs. But, like me, she justified it, not because of God's word, but because she didn't think she could survive without her man. The reality that children will go into the system while a mother seeks help or that she will have to trust her children to strangers far outweighs the physical pain she endures. What women don't see is with each beating, it escalates, and in time, the next one may be the last.

First of all, most women in generational poverty have never seen a good outcome for them or their children. Restraining orders are a joke. Nothing will protect them from a drug or alcohol induced rage, gangs, or just sheer meanness. I have learned that is true across the board. So, nothing is reported, nothing is done, and the cycle continues with children watching on. Children mimic what they see, not what happens to them physically. They see with their eyes and process and then act it out themselves. Those acts of violence are burned into their psyche, and unless they are mentored and shown the difference, history will repeat itself.

In my Bible it says in Genesis that God created woman from the side of a man, not his foot. God saw that man needed a companion, not a servant. Eve walked alongside Adam in the garden and had fellowship with God; she wasn't left out and then Adam came home to tell her what God said and how she should respond. God said they would be "one flesh". How on earth can a man justify beating a woman? Isn't that like whaling on himself? God's plan was for perfect unity in the male-female relationship and in creation. We have just spent several thousand years watering things down, but there you have it.

Here's the second part of Paul's writing to the Ephesians about marriage. (Ephesians 5:25 – 26)

"Husbands, love your wives, as Christ loved the church and gave Himself up for her, that he might sanctify her, having cleansed her by the washing of water with the word, so that he might present the church to Himself in splendor, without spot or wrinkle or any such thing, that she might be holy and without blemish. _In the same way husbands should love their wives as their own bodies. He who loves his wife loves himself. For no one ever hated his own flesh, but nourishes and cherishes it, just as Christ does the church_."

God said that...not me.

"God whispers to us in our pleasures, speaks to us in our conscience, but shouts in our pains: It is His megaphone to rouse a deaf world."

CS Lewis

CHAPTER 13

My husband violated parole and went to prison. When he came back home, the beatings became more frequent and much worse. I was hospitalized more times than I can count with broken ribs, black eyes, busted lips. Just like what happened with my dad, the anger was building, and one day I snapped and fought back. I hit him in the head with a cast iron skillet and stabbed him in the eye with a kitchen knife. The police were called by neighbors and since he was so wounded, the police placed me in handcuffs and charged me with assault. Thankfully, he did not press charges.

I was spiraling down. I quit my job. I left MY apartment and moved in with a friend. Tweety was with her godparents. In three months, I went back to work and back to him. He attended anger management classes, and I thought there might be a possibility for our marriage, but by then, I was so angry.

Not even a month later, I received a phone call from a girl who said she was pregnant by my husband. It was a Tuesday. I went to legal aid and filed for divorce the next day. I got everything done myself and brought the papers home to him. He looked at me and cried. Did he love me? I don't' know. Did he really care for me? Maybe, as much as he could for anyone. But I knew this was not living and I needed out. And when I left, for the first time in my life, I felt free.

I moved out of the apartment and rented a house in the same neighborhood. I took a job working in the day care at a Baptist Church downtown. Tweety was ten years old by now. I was 24 and exhausted. I went to Parkland and told them I wanted my tubes tied. They refused because of my age. I was persistent, and they said if I took a class, they would do the procedure. I took a one-day class and had my tubes tied the next day. I didn't want any more children. I was so tired. I was a single, working mother with a little girl who needed me. We had both been through so much, and I knew how blessed I was to have a healthy, safe, beautiful daughter. I did not want to do anything to jeopardize our life. I could not afford to give her what she needed much less another child. I made the right decision.

BUT GOD

What I did doesn't happen too often. By now, I was 24 years old, and in spite of all the negative experience I had survived, Tweety had been sheltered for the most part. My wonderful friend, whose parents were Tweety's godparents, took their role in her life seriously. They helped her and in doing so, helped me take the necessary steps I needed to take to keep her safe. I knew that having another child would put all of that at risk, and I feared being at the mercy of a new "baby daddy." That life was behind me and it was going to be me and Tweety from this point forward.

Some people applaud and call me "responsible". Others say I was selfish. I do know I did what I could physically and mentally handle at the time. God knew what was in my future and the battles I would soon face. Even though I wasn't in a relationship with God at the time, I know He was part of my decision or rather, my thought process. To say that one woman should not have children because of their economic state is paramount to playing God. If we truly believe children are from God, then who is anyone to say a woman should not have children because of her socio-economic status? Yes, we need to educate and help our women understand what a family looks like and the benefits of education. Yes, there are a ton of obstacles to work through and problems to overcome. But, judging these women and telling them they should not have children is not for anyone to decide but the woman and God. Are there consequences if she cannot care for her children? Yes. Should there be? Yes. But, the better approach is to meet her where she is, don't judge her, and give her help and build a support system around her. (I sound like a broken record, don't I!)

God is always showing examples of caring for single women or widows. The Jewish culture was very in tune with making sure women without husbands were cared for and their children were part of a family. Jesus knew that a poor woman in His society and her children were at risk unless a family member cared for them and took them into their household. What does all of this mean? Well, Jesus was born into a world of poverty. The Jews were under Roman rule and were very poor. They were practically slaves. Famine was everywhere. Yet children, even in the direst of circumstances, were always welcome and treasured...by Jesus Himself. If He didn't cast judgment, how can we?

"I do not at all understand the mystery of Grace - only that it meets us where we are, but does not leave us where it found us."

Anne Lamott

CHAPTER 14

I didn't date at all. I started going to church with Tweety, and we became more and more involved. As I started to hear God, the walls of distrust, anger, and bitterness started coming down. I began to understand and believe Jesus would never hurt me, abandon me, and that He loved me...just as I am. For years I had lived in guilt and shame. I believed somehow all the awful things that had happened may have been my fault, or, that I could have done something.... anything to make it better. But, that all changed when I met Jesus. It all changed when I understood His forgiveness and there was nothing I could ever say or do to lose His love and grace. I gave my life to Christ at age 25 and have never looked back.

My new life in Christ filled me and gave me hope. I had a new joy and new energy. I began teaching a women's mission class and facilitating a Bible study in my home. I participated in the kid's ministry alongside Tweety. Our life was centered on God and our church, and we were happy. My church body wrapped their arms around Tweety and me and cared for us and loved us. They welcomed us into their church with open arms. It wasn't too long before nothing gave me more joy than helping others through hard times and spending time in God's word and with His people.

BUT GOD

God is the answer for the hurting, the abused, rich, poor....HE is the answer. God changed my life, and I know He was with me all along. He was there is many of my decisions, my drive to keep going, the people He placed in my life to help. There is no doubt in my mind God has been with me from the very beginning. When those walls were broken by His love, I was changed. The world grew from my isolated relationships into a big church family. They poured their love (God's love) into my life through Bible study, discipleship training, fellowship with one another, and community. It was a place I felt safe. It was the first time I felt safe in a group. It didn't happen overnight, but over time this congregation proved through their actions that their love was real and founded in Christ. Their actions spoke louder than words. I could see Jesus in so many people, in how they lifted each other up in prayer, took care of each other, and loved each other. Church was a safe haven and a place I could be free, really free from fear, anger, and doing all the heavy lifting myself. God and His church came alongside me, and all I knew from that point on was I wanted to give back.

The Apostle Paul talks about the Macedonian church as an example of giving. "We want you to know, brothers about the grace of God that has been given among the churches of Macedonia, for in a severe test of affliction, their abundance of joy and their extreme poverty have overflowed in a wealth of generosity on their part. For they gave according to their means, as I can testify, and beyond their means, of their own accord, begging us earnestly for the favor of taking part in the relief of the saints...and this, not as we expected, but they "gave themselves first to the Lord, and they by the will of God to us." (II Corinthians 8:1-5.)

This kind of giving, this kind of church is the way my church was, and that example led me to follow Jesus and give my life to serving Him.

"Who, being loved, is poor?"

Oscar Wilde

CHAPTER 15

Tweety was a teenager. She was a great student; she was beautiful and setting goals for her life. She was a great child. God was blessing us in so many ways I could have never imagined. I haven't said a whole lot about Tweety, and I think this is a good place to talk about her. After all, even though when she was born, I had no idea what to do with myself; not to mention a baby! But, she turned out to be the one good thing in my life that drove me to succeed. There was no way I was going to let this child grow up like I did. She was the sole reason I pushed myself forward. She was not going to worry about where she would sleep, if she would eat, or being abused. She was not going to live in fear.

Like I said, when she was a baby, she was the star. Her grandmother and her godmother took care of her and loved her...and spoiled her. She was always in church. They made sure of it.

Tweety did grow up in day care. When she was a toddler her teachers said she had "behavior issues". Those issues turned out to be she was too "busy." She was always looking for something to do and she would bully the other kids at times. I really didn't think much of it at the time. I was working too hard, and she didn't behave that way at home.

As she grew a little older and started school, she began to show signs of anger and resentment. She was very active in all sports and was outgoing. I was actively involved in her school and PTA. I made sure school was her number one priority, and she participated in all school related activities. When she was ten, we found out she needed glasses. She had not been able to see anything well for a long time and I had no idea. (She didn't either.) I thought the glasses might help, but, at that age, kids have no mercy when it comes to teasing and I was fearful she would be teased or bullied like I was. When she got glasses, it was apparent she had not been able to see for a long time. It opened up a whole new world for her and she was happy with them. I thought it would solve her problem with depression and anger. It didn't. We had a heart to heart one day and It turns out she was angry that I couldn't come eat lunch with her at school like the other mothers, and I wasn't able to go on field trips or come to her school parties due to my work. As a mother, it's hard to explain why I couldn't risk losing my job. This is about the age she started to ask about her dad. That was another subject I wasn't ready to talk about as well. I gave her as much information as a ten year- old can process, but she really surprised me. Her questions were more about why I stayed with abusive men. Why did I allow it? All this time, I thought I had hidden the ugliness from her. She knew.

I was "military" in the way I raised her. We were not BFF's. She knew my role and she knew hers. She was not allowed to go to sleepovers because I didn't trust anyone with her and, we didn't have the money for bowling, movies, skating, and all the other things kids her age were doing. I also couldn't get her there and pick her up. I was not going to risk her safety to anyone, and I trusted no one other than her godparents.

Her depression escalated and turned into rebellion. She would cuss at her teachers and act out in class. This had never happened before. We went to counseling together. The counselor said she was suffering from "only child syndrome." I had kept her from cousins, other family, and an active social life. I had to explain some things about my life to help her understand why. In the setting of a good counselor, we had an open dialogue about my life and experiences. It was a lot for her to take in even though I left out quite a bit, but, she understood and seemed to put all of it behind her so she could move forward.

When she was 15, she became a VBS team lead at "Mercy Street." She met a great young lady who became her mentor. Tweety embraced this ministry and began pouring into her friends lives and encouraged them to refrain from sex and self-destructive behavior, but rather to grow in Christ. At 16, they took a retreat to Austin. They were allowed to take a blanket and a book. No cell phone, no electronics...only a book and a blanket. They spent the night on the street. They literally slept on the sidewalk and experienced, just for a minute, what it was like to be homeless. Tweety came back from the retreat and for the first time told me she understood a little of what I had been through. It changed the direction of her life.

From that point forward Tweety went into high gear. I was adamant about education, but I didn't need to be. She was driven to succeed in school. She continued to play on all sports teams and is still friends with some of her teammates today. She made friends easily and was well liked. She was an excellent student and graduated with honors with a scholarship for college. She is now studying for a degree in HR and Non-Profit management. She also has a dream to become a baker (she loves to bake...not sure where that came from!) I was (am) so proud of her!

She dated a young man for about three years. She was in college and he was as well. He dropped out and wanted her to quit school and come live with him. She said no, and he moved on. She is confident, when the time is right, the right man will come into her life.

Today, Tweety is 21 years old, in school on a scholarship, working and supporting herself, and on the way to a career she has chosen. She was born fourth generation poverty and today she is first generation removed from poverty. She is thriving! Her faith in the Lord is strong, and I know He is going to use her in a mighty way.

Tweety and I are close. She told me not long ago that the best thing I ever gave her was encouraging her to rely on her faith in times of trouble and to turn to God always when things are tough. As a mother, I am so blessed. Yes, God has wonderful plans for Tweety, and I am so thankful He gave her to me. What an amazing gift! He knew all along!

BUT GOD

When you are struggling to make it every day and you have your nose down trying to avoid all the land mines, you miss a lot. Tweety blossomed into a beautiful woman, and I missed so much. I focused so much on making sure we had provisions that I think I may have missed some good memories, but God had it the whole time. He had people in our lives to help this precious girl along when I couldn't. Good people, who loved the Lord, were placed strategically along my path and her path to help us sidestep some of those landmines. I can look back and see His hand and His protection over us. At the time, I thought it was all my effort. But when I see my life through His eyes, I clearly see He was there all along.

"For I know the plans I have for you, declares the Lord, plans for welfare and not for evil, to you a future and a hope. Then you will call upon me and come and pray to me, and I will hear you. You will seek me and find me, when you seek me with all your heart." (Jeremiah 29:11-13)

"Faith sees the invisible, Believes the unbelievable, and receives the impossible."

Corrie Ten Boom

CHAPTER 16

In March 2010, I started a new chapter with a new job in logistics. Like every other position I have had, I started at the bottom in the warehouse and within a year had worked my way up to dispatch. This is the time God brought Kevin into my world. Kevin was a driver who lived in New York. I was only a voice in his ear for a long time. His route brought him through Dallas and after all that time on the phone, we finally met. He asked me out right away but to his disappointment, I turned him down.

Later, I called him and explained. I explained where I was in life and that I wasn't ready to date. To my surprise, he said he would wait. What guy does that? Really! We continued to be friends for the next 6 ½ years. We talked on the phone all the time, and when he asked me out again, I said yes. Kevin and I continued a long-distance friendship. I was actually in a good place. I had a steady job, Tweety was doing well, we had a roof over our head and food to eat. God was in my life, and I actually thought I could stop and catch my breath.

It was during this time I felt a painful lump in my left breast. I went to my doctor and had a mammogram. It was cancer. The first person I called was Kevin. I told him, "Guess what I found out today?" He was expecting good news, I think. "I have breast cancer." He was completely shocked. When he asked what I was going to do, my response was, "get through this and move forward." He prayed for me and even though I told him I was confident everything would be fine, I was melting on the inside. How?

About a week later, I took a call from the doctor at work. I went into the lady's room for privacy and thought no one was in there. We talked about my choices and what my treatment plan would look like. To my surprise, I wasn't alone in the lady's room. An HR employee was in there and heard the entire conversation. You would think there would be a little compassion. A week later, the company laid me off. It wasn't a massive lay off, just me.

I was devastated and broke down for the first time. I truly didn't know what to do next. Of all the things I had survived, of all the pain and hardship I had dealt with and kept going, I did not know if I had what it would take to make it through this hurdle. I would need a double mastectomy followed by a year of chemotherapy. I had no job. I had no money. I prayed. Oh, how I prayed...but, I didn't feel confident anymore.

BUT GOD

Prayer is an amazing gift from our God, but, it can sometimes be frustrating. We can know in our head that God hears us, and we can know in our heart that He loves us...but sometimes, when you are alone in the dark with God, and your heart is literally breaking, and fear is hitting every nerve, and you are begging God to help you...and you hear "nothing." Nothing but stillness, nothing but empty air all around, and the weight of the darkness relentlessly pushes you to the floor...I was in that place. I could not just "get through this and move forward." I had been sucker punched at work, I had a horrible diagnosis that would keep me sick for at least a year (if I survived), and I felt there was no future. What would I do? What would Tweety do? I did not have that peace which passes understanding, and my faith was taking a nose dive.

I guess I could go to a shelter, but shelter life is no picnic. Dallas has good ones. But the rule is you can eat and sleep there at night, but you have to leave during the day. You cannot just lie around and do nothing. The hope is you will go out and find work. There are people there to help in that respect, but often, the mentally ill and addicts only want a place to sleep. If you are caught with drugs or are drunk and/or high, you cannot stay. Mom would take us to shelters every now and then in California, but we never stayed more than a night or two and the shelters there were dirty and terrible for small children. Here in Dallas, most are pretty nice and if you live thirty consecutive days in a shelter, you are automatically eligible for Section 8 housing, and the shelter is required to find housing for you.

But, I was sick. I couldn't work and go to Chemo. So, this was not an option.

I remembered Jesus in the Garden. "Let this cup pass from me...not my will but your will be done." He was thinking of us (you and me) in His darkest hour. He would be abandoned by everyone he knew, including his disciples and family. He would be beaten, spit on, mocked, go through an unjust, unlawful trial, He would be flogged and then stripped naked and nailed to a cross for all to see...He would do all of this for me. But then...His triumph over death. He reveals Himself as the risen Lord and all of Hell, Satan, and His demons are defeated once and for all. He rises from the dead and is glorified to take His place at the right hand of God. WOW.

I am convinced, now, that the bigger the problem, the bigger the obstacle...the bigger the miracle God has planned. Just wait. That is what I did. It's all I could do.

"There is no surprise more magical that the surprise of being loved. It is God's finger on man's shoulder."

Charles Morgan

CHAPTER 17

I called Kevin. "Guess what happened to me today?" Kevin wasn't about to bite again. "I lost my job." The walls came down and the tears flowed. Kevin was calm, he listened, and then he said the most beautiful words I had ever heard. He said, "Baby, God has been working on me and He is telling me I need to care for you and help you through this." But how, I wondered.

"I am going to move to Dallas. I have a friend I can live with and I will work out of Dallas and take care of you while you are sick. We are going through this together."

I was so grateful, but it scared me to death. No one, or no man, had ever done anything for me just because he cared and loved me. What was this going to cost me? Isn't it funny how when God answers a prayer, when He hears our cries, we are all shocked and in disbelief when He answers us!

Kevin came to Dallas as promised. He took care of me as I went through a double mastectomy followed by chemotherapy for the next year. He was there to help me through the fever, chills, nausea, the loss of all my hair...there isn't anything pretty about cancer. He made sure my bills were paid on time, and I never missed a single one. Kevin never asked for anything in return. I had never felt worthy of someone caring for me so much. I had never been loved as a person. My only question was why?

I thought for sure Kevin would go back to New York after I began to heal. He didn't. Instead, he asked me to marry him. Now, obviously this man loved me. He had seen me at my absolute worst. During those long hours of being sick, I shared my life with him…. the good, the bad, and the ugly. It didn't scare him! Wow. No one had ever treated me this well ,. and I truly didn't know how to accept this kind of love.

Obviously, I said yes. Kevin is now my husband, my friend, my partner, my number one supporter, and is a gift directly from God for me and is my miracle, my answer to the prayers I made when I was so lost and alone. Now, Kevin isn't perfect; but after what I have been through and the men I have been with, he is as close to it as I can imagine and when he isn't, we work through it.

And, oh, by the way. "Vengeance is mine" says the Lord. The company that let me go after they found out I was sick…. well, I didn't need to sue them (like many thought I should have.) They imploded on themselves and went out of business. So, while I used all my energy in my battle with cancer, God took care of them in a way I could not.

BUT GOD

I emerged from yet another battle with cancer with a new energy I had not known before. God was filling me with joy and I loved life, for real. He had brought me through another storm and was shining His light on me and through me as never before. Cancer was another miracle in disguise.

Cancer, in its evil effort to destroy life, was used by God for His glory. I praise Him all the more because of the victory through Him and for the burning passion inside of me to be His servant and to be a witness of His love to everyone I meet.

"The steadfast love of the Lord never ceases; His mercy never comes to an end. It is new every morning. Great is Thy faithfulness! "The Lord is my portion," says my soul; therefore, I will hope in Him." The Lord is good to those who wait for Him, to the soul who seeks Him. It is good that one should wait quietly for the salvation of the Lord." (Lamentations 3: 22-26)

"We must talk about poverty because people insulated by their own comfort, lose sight of it."

Dorothy Day

CHAPTER 18

After my battle with breast cancer, I took another job in dispatch. But God had other plans. I had been walking my neighborhood and noticed these white people planting a "farm" in the neighborhood. Me, being the "need to know what's happening "kind of person I am, went over to see what was going on. When I learned it was a ministry to produce good nutritious food and create jobs for the men living in South Dallas - Bonton, this thought flashed in my mind...what about the women? Most of the population in our neighborhood consists of single mothers and children. What about them?

Then God spoke. That's your job, Chocolate. This is what I have been preparing you for your whole life. These women need you. They need your story. They need ME in their lives to give them the peace, strength, grace, and mercy you have received in your life. You are my anointed one to reach into their lives and be my messenger. WOW, really? Just how am I supposed to do that? (Don't ever ask God that question unless you want the answer...look at Moses, David, Esther, Ruth and Naomi, Rahab, Deborah, Paul, Peter, Mary...there are so many examples of God taking the most ill-equipped people and using them to bring glory to Him in ways they never could achieve... the answer to that question is always a miracle!)

I looked back over the brokenness in my life. I looked at my mom with eight children, still on drugs and on the streets, now with AIDS. I looked at my Dad, he too with eight children, still an alcoholic and no change in his life at all. What saved me from that life? What carried me the whole time (even when I didn't even know it?) GOD. JESUS. He alone is the difference.

So, I said ok God. Here I am. What do I do next?

What came next has been nothing short of a miracle. God brought the resources, the training, the people in my life I needed, just as he did before and I didn't even know it! Everything was provided to clear the path for me to be His servant to the women in Bonton and to women outside of my neighborhood. I formed Redeemed Women in May 2017, and the blessings continue to pour on me and those I serve. The passion is growing each day, and God shows up mightily every day. In less than a year we have managed to start discipleship training, have a group of women who meet for fellowship that are forming bonds of friendship, a woman gave her life to Christ, another wants to step up and be a leader in our community, an anonymous donor gave us a brand new van to take ladies to doctors appointments, the grocery, job interviews, classes, and the list goes on! God has placed every resource I need and continues to build this ministry, and I believe with every breath He has mighty plans for the lives of the women I serve! I cannot wait to see what He is going to do. South Dallas - Bonton will be the city on a hillside whose light is seen in a hurting world...and people will be drawn to the light and lives will be forever changed. Amen.

"The Spirit of the Lord is upon me, because the Lord has anointed me to bring good news to the poor; he has sent me to bind up the brokenhearted, to proclaim liberty to the captives, and the opening of the prison to those who are bound; to proclaim the year of the Lord's favor, and the day of vengeance of our God; to comfort all who mourn; to grant to those who mourn in Zion; to give them a beautiful headdress instead of ashes, the oil of gladness instead of mourning, the garment of praise instead of a faint spirit; that they may be called oaks of righteousness, planting of the Lord, that He may be glorified."

(Isaiah 61:1-3)

EPILOGUE

Today, Redeemed Women, led by Chocolate, is actively serving women in South Dallas and the Bonton neighborhood. She is on the front lines, "boots on the ground" daily, meeting needs and walking hand in hand with women in dire need of not just physical help; but also kindness and consistency in their lives. Chocolate gives the gift of relationship and friendships grow. The door opens for God's light to shine through her and lives are being changed. She is quickly becoming known as the "lady who can help," whether it be a ride to the grocery, doctor, or social security office (in our new van, "Vanna White!"), or, a bag of necessities from the shed stocked in her back yard. She has come alongside her neighbors and walked through their pain and listened to their stories. She visits with them in their homes, she meets them where they are, to listen and share God's word with them. She has an arsenal of partners equipped to handle any need she might not be able to provide; however, she does not simply "hand them over"; she remains by their side.

There is so much more Redeemed Women can do and plans to do. Because Chocolate was obedient to God's call, the door is wide open, and the time is right for us to share God's love to a hurting community and help them rebuild from the inside out! We are confident this is just the beginning! We share a vision of transformation and restoration in South Dallas. Please join us! *Your prayers are the most powerful gift you can give. But,* if you would like to support us through monthly giving or a one-time gift, we can promise your gift will go directly to help the women we serve. If you would like to donate to the shed, go to our website and click on the link for Amazon. We keep a list of items we need to keep on hand and update it regularly. There are many ways to serve and as we grow, we will make those known on our web site, Facebook, or Instagram ("friend us" @redeemedwomendallas) Join us and make a difference in the lives of women who need you and your support! They are your neighbors too. Together, let's love them well!

Our Mission
"Transforming women to lead independent lives by building relationships and addressing their spiritual, physical, and vocational needs."

Web site: www.redeemedwomen.org
E-mail: chocolate@redeemedwomen.org
Phone: 469.215.3400

May God's Blessings be on You .....